Robert Maass

When Autumn Comes

Scholastic Inc.

NEW YORK   TORONTO
LONDON   AUCKLAND   SYDNEY

ISBN 0-590-96825-4

12 11 10 9 8 7 6   0 1/0

Printed in the U.S.A.   08

First Scholastic printing, September 1996

When summer ends and autumn comes,
it's time to put on sweaters and long pants.

Birds fly south to warmer places.

Boats are pulled up onto shore.

School has just begun
when autumn comes.
Old friends are together
and new friends are made.

Autumn is a time for making ready—for painting

and fixing

and changing
and airing.

It's a time
of preparation.

Wood is cut,
gathered,
and stacked in cords.

A chimney sweep
brushes away soot
inside the chimney
so fires will burn well.

Leaves turn red,
orange, yellow, brown,
painting the ground
as they fall.
They're raked up
so grass can grow
in the spring,
and to make great
jumping-into piles.

The farmer knows
that autumn's here.
He reaps and threshes
and stores the
late feed corn.
Lambs' woolly coats
grow thick.

Apples ripen.
Cider is pressed

and taken home.

Indian corn decorates
the season.
Pumpkins are harvested
from the fields.
Halloween is coming soon.

Pumpkin people
spring up on lawns.
It's time to dress up,
trick-or-treat,
and be spooky.

Days grow shorter
and shadows stretch.
By now there are just
a few more nuts to store.

When the first
frost comes,
the cold
is easy to see.

At Thanksgiving, families gather to feast
and to remember the good things of the year.

Then caps and boots and heavy coats are taken out.
Winter's at our heels

as autumn ends.